Music Journal

This book belongs to

....

....

Music is life.
That's why our hearts
have beats.

Made in the USA
Middletown, DE
13 September 2024

60898351R00070